A BOOK OF COURTESY

A BOOK OF COURTESY

THE ART OF LIVING WITH YOURSELF AND OTHERS

SISTER M. MERCEDES, O.P.
REVISED BY HER STUDENTS,
DOMINICAN CONVENT UPPER SCHOOL

HarperSanFrancisco
A Division of HarperCollins*Publishers*

HarperCollins books may be purchased for educational, business, or sales promotional use. For information please write: Special Markets Department, HarperCollins Publishers Inc., 10 East 53rd Street, New York, NY 10022.

HarperCollins Web site: http://www.harpercollins.com
HarperCollins®, ♨®, and HarperSanFrancisco™ are
trademarks of HarperCollins Publishers Inc.

FIRST EDITION

Library of Congress Cataloging-in-Publication Data
Mary Mercedes, Sister.
A book of courtesy : the art of living with yourself and others / Sister Mary Mercedes ; revised by her students. — 1st ed.
p. cm.
ISBN 0–06–251758–9 (alk. paper)
I. Courtesy. II. Title.
BJ1533.C9 M34   2001
395—dc21   00–054166

01 02 03 04 05 ❖/RRD 10 9 8 7 6 5 4 3 2 1

IN MEMORY OF
SISTER MARY MERCEDES, O. P.,
WHO WROTE THE ORIGINAL *BOOK OF COURTESY*,
AND SISTER MARY MAURICE, O.P.,
WHO TAUGHT US THE ART OF LIVING
WITH OURSELVES AND OTHERS

This book was revised in 2000 by students of Sister Mary Mercedes, O.P., from the class of 1950 at the Dominican Convent Upper School, San Rafael, California:

Pamela Thorsen Amoss
Carol Monpere Becker
Mary Helen Briscoe
Ellen Buckley
Emalee Sala Chapman
Lillian Machado Dickson
Margaret Marks Grasso
Virginia Stewart Jarvis
Joan English Lane
Isabelle Surcouf Manning
Lynn Barry Pickart
Angela Musco Putkey
Ardath Graber Rouas
Dorris Callaghan Slater
Sister Mary Gervaise Valpey, O.P.

FOR OUR GRANDDAUGHTERS AND GRANDSONS
WITH LOVE

CONTENTS

INTRODUCTION

෴

"A book about . . . *courtesy?*" said a friend when she heard I was writing this introduction. To her the word seemed arcane, quaint; it spoke to another time. This friend, however, had never studied under the Dominicans. She had not been exposed to the exquisite code of civility that they tried to imprint on each of us students. So I had to explain to her what "courtesy" meant.

From that explanation came this introduction.

Some people are born knowing how to live, knowing from the start what it takes to become a worthy human being. It is as if they have it stamped somewhere on their DNA: "Love your neighbor as yourself. Do unto others as you would have them do unto you." Sister Mercedes Lane was one of those people. It was her work to teach life lessons to hundreds upon hundreds of adolescent girls; later, through a ripple-in-the-pond effect, to their children and the children of their children.

She came from a powerful tradition. The Dominicans have always been teachers, devoted to education since the order was founded in France in 1207 A.D. A century and a half ago, when California's bishop called for volunteers to open a convent and school in the fledgling state, a Dominican nun was the only one to come forward. The intrepid Mother

Mary Goemaere sailed from France in 1849, crossed the Isthmus of Panama on the back of a mule, and arrived in California in the midst of the gold rush. She brought with her a commitment to excellence and a much-needed code of behavior, all of it framed in a joyous religious faith. In 1850 Mother Mary Goemaere founded what is now the oldest independent school in California, now known as the San Domenico School, in San Anselmo.

Sister Mercedes joined the order a generation or so later. Gifted with a sympathetic view of the world, she eventually put that worldview into words. She called the work *A Book of Courtesy.* First published nearly a century ago (around 1910), it has been updated several times in the years since.

By the time our class came on the scene in 1946, the book had taken on the dimension of legend. Upperclassmen assured us that our small courtesy book was second in importance only to the New Testament, that it contained a code of conduct covering every challenge imaginable, from one's first day in a new school to, years later, the menu for one's first dinner party. Here were rules for birth and death. Here were rules for everything in between.

The *real* book of courtesy (we discovered when we finally got our own copies from the bookstore) was far more modest in its aspirations. Perusing it, we teenagers soon recognized that we were on to something unique. Nothing here of the perfunctory protocol found in etiquette books previously forced upon us; this book, instead, made a deep appeal to our budding humanity.

Courtesy, it told us, involves a special skill: the ability to put oneself in someone else's place in order to see what is needed in any situation. These words read fresh and true to us then. They still do. Like so many other graduates, long after we moved out into the world and had children of our own, that book stayed with us.

The nun who wrote it did as well.

"Never let it be said of you, 'She is a snob.' Snobs never entertain angels unawares. They care only for those from whom they can get something. Snobs measure most things by money."

Sister Mercedes wrote that nearly a century ago. I recently met a woman sixty-two years out of Dominican who can still quote it verbatim.

"When you take a piece of bread, always break it on the bread plate." "A young woman should always sit in curves." Admirable goals all, and we tried to adhere to them (though I never quite understood that last one). Just as strong as her admonishments were the memories she left. "She was always so aware and so prayerful," remembers Leila Rowson Brown, class of 1949. Others recall her watchful eye in study hall and the refectory: "She had eyes in the back of her head," laughs

Nancy Weston, '39, who was caught one lunchtime trying to flip her butter pat onto the ceiling. "And I was so sure she was looking the other way."

She seemed to be everywhere, moving in silent majesty up and down the halls, recalls a student from the 1930s. One day the girl encountered her outside the upstairs dorm. Sister Mercedes glided past, paused, and tapped her on the shoulder: "You could improve your top drawer," she said. She was about to continue on her way when, concerned perhaps that she might have humbled the girl too much, she added, "But you do have excellent posture."

Several years ago some of us in the class of 1950, realizing that we would soon be marking the fiftieth anniversary of our graduation, decided to celebrate our return with a special gift for the community. A gift that would acknowledge the continuity of a great school and at the same time offer something tangible to present and past students, to their children and grandchildren. One evening two former classmates, Lillian Machado Dickson and Pamela Thorsen Amoss, were sitting by the fire talking of family and schooling when they came up with an idea. Why not take Sister Mercedes' courtesy book and update it for the new century? And why offer it only to the Dominican family? The need for civility and good manners is certainly universal. Although fashions may change, true courtesy does not. Its spirit is timeless.

So we handed out assignments. Class members worked on individual chapters and added several new ones ("Electronic Communications," for instance). Isabelle Surcouf Manning then put all of the material together and edited it into a final draft.

Herewith, the class of 1950—fifty years older, somewhat wiser—offers you a new version of the inestimable *Book of Courtesy*.

Carol Monpere, '50

Love your neighbor as yourself,
and do unto others as you would have them do unto you.
—*Galatians 5:14*

I

A SYMPATHETIC MANNER

〰

*Y*ou may not think that living with others is an art, but it is the finest and most difficult of arts. By learning it early in life, you can save yourself many unpleasant experiences.

You can master this art only if you treat others with courtesy. Courtesy is a way of living inspired by thoughtfulness, consideration, and respect for others and for yourself.

We all know people who, upon entering a room, bring with them a cloud. But we also know those whose arrival always brings sunshine. A Boston daily paper once carried this item: "Yesterday was dark and rainy, but Philip Brooks passed down Newspaper Row and the sun shone."

Some people are totally insensitive to others and are constantly ruffling their feelings. They make jokes about other people's appearance or embarrass their companions with sarcastic remarks and unkind criticism.

Others would never ruffle your feelings, but their manner is cold and they leave you cold. They seem to have no

1

interest in you, not a glint of sympathy for your joys and sor-rows; they never cheer you up and they often leave you feel-ing downhearted.

Some find it difficult to relate to others. They may make constant demands on your time, calling and asking you to help with their problems, but they abandon you when you need them. They are self-centered and can think only of their own needs and desires.

Have you ever, in a burst of temper, wounded those you love best in the world, or spoken words that you would give anything to take back? You cannot live amicably with others until you have learned to control your temper. All it takes is making a habit of holding your temper instead of letting it control you.

The intolerant person is unable to see another's point of view. This person demands that others look through his eyes and think that any other perspective is wrong. Such a person is hard to live with, as are those who are determined to have their own way at all times.

Consideration is the heart of good manners, and a cour-teous manner is a grace that every young person should acquire. Sympathy, sensitivity, and tact make you a desirable companion at home, in school, and at work. Conveying your support through a sympathetic smile or a friendly touch can help a friend through a bad time. Tactful behavior springs from the heart, from the desire to put others at ease and make them comfortable, even in awkward or difficult situations.

Some people proudly claim that they do not wish to be tactful because tact is not "honest." They do not realize that their "honesty" can often be cruel; you can wound others with tactless or insensitive remarks, making the world more difficult for them and for yourself.

There is more kindness in the world than you may believe. What passes for a lack of sympathy can simply be a lack of imagination or a lack of self-confidence; perhaps you hesitate to intrude upon another's joy or sorrow. Fearing the hurt of rejection, you may cloud another's joy by seeming indifferent, or leave another's sorrow uncomforted because you fear your own feelings.

If you are slow of speech or shy, remember that a sympathetic manner, a smile, a mere friendly touch can help smooth the rough edges of life. If you let the right moment pass today, or if you recognize the hurt you have caused only after the fact, you can still learn from your mistakes.

When we become aware of our own shortcomings, we can more readily understand and forgive the faults of others. Despite our many differences, every one of us shares the same humanity with its strengths and its weaknesses.

"Instill your love into all the world, for a good character is what is remembered," wrote a king of Heracleopolis to his son and successor, Merikare, c. 2135–2040 B.C.

A friend may well be reckoned the masterpiece of Nature.
—*Ralph Waldo Emerson (1803–1882)*

II

FRIENDSHIPS

❧

*O*ne of the most helpful influences in our lives is a good friendship. Although youth is the time when many transforming friendships are made, and our most enduring ones, we continue to forge new attachments throughout our lives. A strong friendship can teach the meaning of unselfishness. A healthy friendship calls for what is best in us and stimulates us to our highest endeavors.

Many young people are mainly influenced by their friends and peer group in school. Their standards and their way of looking at life are determined chiefly by their companions and associates in matters of dress, speech, and behavior. This is evident from the greater weight that young people place upon the approval of their peers rather than their elders.

The person who knows himself and his imperfections needs to be careful that it is not by his weaknesses that he attracts his friends, but by his strengths. Many men and women may be more popular than he is, and some of them deserve their popularity. Others have achieved popularity, however, without deserving it, because amiable weaknesses can seem more attractive than sterling worth. As Eleanor Roosevelt (1884–1962) said, "No one can make you feel inferior without your consent." The popular individual may appear to be more fun than the disciplined professional or the serious person with a definite goal, but associating with him may not be constructive and may lead you into trouble.

In order to grow, friendships need loyalty, love, mutual consideration, and willingness to see the other's point of view. You choose your pleasures, your books, and your occupations, but you do not choose your friends; you only discover them.

The knowledge of having a friend and of being one is the greatest blessing life affords. Perhaps no one can tell you how to make friends, since friends are born, not made; therefore, it is worthwhile to put forth your best effort to make yourself worthy of having good friends.

Cheerfulness keeps up a kind of daylight in the mind,
and fills it with a steady and perpetual serenity.
—Joseph Addison (1672–1719)

III

DAILY COURTESIES

The power to gain friends may in great measure depend on a happy disposition, but the power to keep them depends largely on loyalty, genuine caring, and acceptance of differences, as well as personal habits of promptness, order, personal neatness, and cheerfulness.

Promptness is a cardinal rule when dealing with others: the person who is late for appointments or keeps people waiting for meetings, classes, or meals is an annoyance and is saying in essence, "I don't care enough about you to be on time."

Personal habits reveal a person's character. A disorderly room reflects a lack of self-respect and organization; this applies to dress and cleanliness as well. The person with self-esteem is neat in his personal appearance, stands and sits up straight, and dresses appropriately for the occasion.

Cheerfulness and good spirits allow you to live with a positive attitude; no one enjoys a grumbler or a complainer. A positive outlook makes you a pleasant companion.

There are times when even the best-intentioned person makes a mistake. Certain words help to ease the blunder: "I'm sorry," "It was my fault," or, "I beg your pardon." "Please excuse me" allows for a graceful exit before leaving the table, the room, or the situation. Saying "I beg your pardon" or "Excuse me" is a must when it is necessary to pass in *front* of another person to get to your seat at the theater and it is absolutely impossible to pass *behind* them.

Good manners depend on a basic knowledge of etiquette. Etiquette embraces the rituals and practices that speak to the question "What am I supposed to do?" During your lifetime the rules of etiquette may change, but courtesy and good manners will always be important.

Nobody can be in good health if he does not have all the time
fresh air, sunshine, and good water.
—Flying Hawk, Oglala Sioux Chief (1852–1931)

Health and fitness are better than any gold,
a robust body than countless riches.
—Ecclesiasticus 30:15

IV

MAINTAINING THE PALACE

❦

The body is the palace of the soul.

To sustain a positive attitude and a sympathetic manner, you need to take the best possible care of your health. This is one of your first responsibilities.

You owe it to yourself as well as to others to follow the basic formula for well-being: plenty of sleep and rest, regular exercise appropriate to your physical condition, lots of fresh fruit and vegetables in your diet, and moderation in all things. It is also important that you drink at least six to eight glasses of water every day. Remember that our bodies consist primarily of water, at least 90 percent. Coffee and soft drinks are *not* substitutes for the water our bodies require.

The best exercises, suitable to everyone and the most adapted to physical limitations, are walking and swimming.

Dancing is a good way to develop coordination, good posture, and a graceful way of moving.

There are many types of enjoyable athletic activities to choose from that will leave you exhilarated and tired, but not exhausted.

To keep your good health, always be willing to care for and about yourself. Self-discipline, self-control, and self-respect are the keys to physical and mental health.

Nothing in the world is single,
All things by a law divine
In one spirit meet and mingle.
—*Percy Bysshe Shelley (1792–1822)*

V

INTRODUCTIONS

The purpose of introductions is to make people known to each other and to make guests feel welcome and comfortable. The exchange of names along with descriptive or interesting information helps conversation begin more easily. Good introductions are helpful acts and remarks that reflect respect and thoughtfulness.

You may find it difficult to make an introduction unless you remember the following guides and customs—a no-fail method to avoid confusion.

Begin by preparing yourself mentally before speaking.

When there is an obvious difference in gender, age, or position between the persons you are introducing, state the following name first:

~ The woman or girl

~ The elder person

~ The dignitary of church or state

In general, boys and men and younger people are the person being introduced, and their name is stated *second*. Here is how the most common pairs of people are introduced:

~ "Sarah (girl), this is Henry (boy)."

~ "Mrs. Dawson (woman), this is Mr. Long (man)."

~ "Mrs. Smith (older person), this is Tom Randolph (younger person)."

~ "Mayor Wilson (government dignitary), this is Harriet Johnson (any person)."

~ "Reverend Cross (church dignitary), this is Betsy Lyons (any person)."

Choose any of the following phrases *to connect* the names of those you are introducing. The phrases are listed in order of formality, from most to least formal, and each phrase implies an unstated "to you."

~ "Mrs. Calhoun, *may I present* Mr. Moller?"

~ "Mrs. Calhoun, *may I introduce* Mr. Moller?"

~ "Mrs. Calhoun, *I want to introduce* Mr. Moller."

~ "Mrs. Calhoun, *this is* Mr. Moller."

To lead into an introduction, you might ask

~ "Mrs. Carson, *have you met* Mr. Fry?"

~ "Mrs. Carson, *do you know* Mr. Fry?"

~ "*Have you met each other yet?*"

Polish your introduction by adding phrases that describe relationships or positions and provide a basis for conversation. The introduction becomes more informative when you say, for example, "Mrs. Carson, this is my neighbor Mr. Fry."

When you are being introduced to someone, greet the new acquaintance with a friendly response such as "Hello," "How do you do?" "It is nice to meet you," or, "I am so glad to meet you."

A handshake between the persons being introduced is an appropriate gesture in the following circumstances:

~ Two men usually shake hands.

~ Two women have the option of shaking hands.

~ When a woman or girl is being introduced to a man or boy, the woman or girl offers her hand first.

~ A man or boy being introduced to a woman or girl shakes hands only if the woman or girl offers her hand first.

~ If the person to whom you are being introduced offers a hand to you, the most courteous gesture, of course, is to shake hands.

~ A host or hostess greets everyone with a handshake.

When saying good-bye after being introduced, one person might add, "I am very glad to have met you," and the other person could respond, "Thank you. It was nice to meet you also." Or one person might say, "I hope to meet you again soon," and the other person might respond, "Thank you. I hope so too."

There are situations to avoid in making introductions.

Young adults should not call elders by their first names unless the elder person invites them to do so. Use the appropriate title, such as Mr. Lane, Mrs. Lane, Colonel Powell, and so forth.

Avoid introducing your peers using first names only. It is preferable to say, "Mother, this is Mary Bryant."

Do not use command introductions, such as "John, meet Andrew" or "John, shake hands with Andrew."

Following some additional guidelines will make introductions natural and habitual.

If you feel uncomfortable making introductions, practice aloud, alone, or with a friend. Smile, keep a friendly manner, maintain eye contact, and speak clearly.

When introducing someone to a small group of three to five persons, say, "I would like everyone to meet Jane Yates. Jane, this is Laura Lightfoot, Andrea Cohen, and Jack Shelton." Remember to use first and last names.

If you are seated, it is always respectful to stand during an introduction to an older person or to your hostess. Men should always stand when introduced to women of all ages.

Introduce yourself when there is no one to do it for you: "Hello, I am Ann Busso. I recently moved to the Bay Area from Boston." If you meet someone who is hesitant about your name, it is most gracious to say quickly, "Hi, Mr. Mattel. I'm Rick Fraser, your son's classmate."

If you forget a name, thus making the introduction impossible, say, "I am sorry. What is your name again, please?" If you mispronounce or use the wrong name, simply apologize and try again.

With a warm, welcoming smile, genuine interest in the person, and an attention to names, you will find that introductions become easy and natural.

Conversation . . . is the art of never appearing a bore, of knowing how to say everything interestingly, to entertain with no matter what, to be charming with nothing at all.
—Guy de Maupassant (1850–1893)

VI

CONVERSATIONS

❧

$\mathcal{C}$onversation, at its best, is a link between mind and mind by which people approach one another with sympathy and enjoyment. It can also be a source of solace and inspiration.

A reciprocal act during which people simply take turns talking *and* listening to each other, your conversation should be stimulating enough to kindle ideas or start an answering train of thought in your listeners. Anyone can learn to be a good listener—that is, a person who listens with interest so as to inspire a lively response.

The greatest irritant in dialogue is interruption; always wait until a natural pause or lull when you are certain the other person has completed his thought before you respond.

Another element of discourse is "small talk," or casual chatting, which is a social skill as well as an ice-breaker. Small talk should be about simple and general topics, like the weather, the surroundings, or the occasion that brings you together.

Because many of us spend a great part of each day in verbal communication, whether it be casual chatting or serious talk, a review of the following guidelines to conversation *and* listening is helpful.

~ Think before you speak, and speak clearly, simply, and sincerely.

~ Say pleasant things with a warm, kind smile while maintaining eye contact.

~ Acknowledge important events in the life of the person with whom you are talking.

~ Pay compliments if deserved, and accept compliments with grace.

~ Change the subject if it appears to be uninteresting or displeasing to the other.

~ If you disagree, do so respectfully.

~ Keep a cheerful frame of mind, develop a sense of humor, and laugh at yourself without putting yourself down.

And now here are ways of conversing that are important to avoid.

~ Do not interrupt or monopolize a conversation by trying to shine with constant witticisms or by rambling on about yourself, your family, or your troubles.

~ Do not be overly opinionated, although you need not agree with everything that other people say merely for the sake of agreeing.

~ Avoid filling in words for the speaker or asking insensitive questions relating, for example, to age, weight, cost of items, or medical issues.

~ Avoid changing a subject in which others are interested.

~ Avoid wounding the feelings of others by making inconsiderate remarks or allusions or by repeating unkind criticisms you have heard. No one appreciates hearing disagreeable things about himself.

~ Never flatter. Praise rings true, but flattery goes beyond the limits of truth and embarrasses its recipient.

~ Never name-drop. Trying to impress makes you sound insecure.

~ Do not complain.

~ Do not give advice unless asked.

~ It is not a duty to be brutally honest.

~ Avoid using slang expressions, never use foul language, and do not replace "Yes" or "No" with "Uh-huh," "Yeah," or "Nope."

Conversation is a creative art as well as an acquired skill. Learn to be entertaining and attentive. Be prepared to talk about interesting topics. Elicit and pursue the ideas and opinions of those with whom you are talking so that the conversation becomes satisfying and even exciting to all involved.

The most important rule to remember is always to ask yourself: Would what I am about to say be of interest to this person or could it hurt anyone?

It is equally wrong to speed a guest who does not want to go,
and to keep one back who is eager. You ought to make welcome
the present guest, and send forth the one who wishes to go.
—Homer (c. 700 B.C.)

VII

COURTESY TO GUESTS

Essential to true hospitality is a generosity of spirit that creates a warm atmosphere and puts the guests at ease by anticipating their needs and encouraging their participation.

If you are seated, always rise and greet courteously any visitors who enter the room.

When you are talking to your elders, it is a good time to practice the art of listening, an essential part of any conversation. Listen thoughtfully in order to make brief comments or to ask questions, as appropriate, that will encourage the guest to continue. Make eye contact and never listen with just one ear, the other attuned to a conversation nearby, or halfheartedly with your attention distracted by your own thoughts or the clouds floating by.

Very often, a guest of your friends or parents will express interest in you and ask questions about your activities. Reply with enthusiasm, but don't go on for too long. You may shift the emphasis from yourself or your interests to any of those indicated by comments and questions from the guest, but do not monopolize the conversation. If it is necessary for you to leave the room when guests are seated, excuse yourself quietly and depart unobtrusively. Never pass between two persons who are talking together.

When you have guests, treat them as you would like to be treated. Whether they are to be with you for an evening, overnight, or for longer, your knowledge of their likes and dislikes can guide you in the arrangements you make for their visit: broccoli or carrots, Fat Head Eddy or Bach, hiking or biking. If you live with others, always consult with your family or roommates before inviting a friend to your house. A discussion with them beforehand will reveal any conflict of schedules and point out how you can be helpful before and during your friend's visit.

Sometimes things can go wrong, or differently than expected. Expressing your distress or embarrassment will make your guest uncomfortable and do nothing to ease the situation. Should your guest suffer a mishap, quickly reassure him, minimize the situation, and graciously accept his apology. Awkward situations and mishaps call for kindhearted responses.

If your guest happens not to like certain dishes served, do not embarrass him by making apologetic comments that call attention to them; merely try unobtrusively to see that he has something else that he prefers.

As a host, you have the responsibility of entertaining your guest, whatever he might like to do, unless your invitation mentioned that you have something to do on your own during part of his visit. Although you may assume that your guest wants to participate in the activities you planned for his stay, be aware of any need he may have for time to himself. On the other hand, courtesy does not allow you the same option.

Refrain from insisting that your guest overstay the time agreed to for his visit or from pressing him with too many attentions. The nicest thing you can do for a guest is to make him feel at home.

*No guest is so welcome in a friend's house that he will not become
a nuisance after three days.*
—Titus Maccius Plautus (254–184 B.C.)

VIII

BEING A GUEST

To be a welcome guest, you must respond promptly to all invitations. (*Invite,* by the way, is a verb, not a noun.) A potentially conflicting engagement is not an excuse to delay your response. Even at the risk of being left without either engagement to enjoy, you must make a choice, respond yes or no, and be prepared to stick by your decision. A prompt response shows your regard and consideration for your host and his efforts to prepare for the event. When declining an invitation, do so without delay to allow the host to invite someone else without giving the impression that he or she is a second choice.

Conflicting invitations from two people can be resolved by accepting the first invitation or declining both. When you must decline, do so with sensitivity, keeping in mind the feelings of the person who invited you.

Generally, the form of your response to an invitation—in person, by telephone, or in an informal note—follows the form of the invitation. In chapter XVII, "Invitations and Responses," there are specific examples of invitations and their responses.

When you have accepted an invitation, show consideration for your host by arriving on time, particularly when dinner is being served, a curtain is going up, or a ride is waiting. When you are invited to an occasion such as a reception, a dance, or a buffet, and for a time within a range—for example, from 6:00 to 9:00 P.M., or an hour clearly after dinner, like 9:00 or 10:00 P.M.—then you may arrive as late as forty-five minutes after the starting time.

When many guests have been invited and arrive nearly at the same time, your host will usually be near the front door to greet them. If he is not, however, you must seek him out to make your presence known.

The most successful occasions are those on which all the guests are enjoying themselves. The ideal guest is thoughtful enough to observe and include other guests who seem shy or not well acquainted.

Do not overstay your welcome. It is important to know when to leave a party, and when an overnight visit or longer stay is over. Leave gracefully without letting yourself be talked into overstaying and without endless good-byes.

Thanking your host as you leave does not excuse you from sending a thank-you note, preferably within a week of your visit. Although it is addressed to your host, it is thoughtful to extend your regards to any family members or house-mates you may have met.

If you are staying overnight with someone who lives with his parents, friends, or roommates, it is nice, although not an obligation, to bring a gift to show your appreciation of their kindness in entertaining you. Gifts that are always welcome include candy, flowers, a bottle of wine, or something you have made yourself. If you are uncertain of what to bring, you might discreetly glance around the house for ideas for a gift that you could send later.

When preparing for your visit, ask your host what activities have been planned, and do your best to bring the appropriate clothes and accessories. Make sure that your belongings are clean and in good condition; don't forget to pack your toothbrush and all the toilet articles you may need so that you won't have to borrow from your host.

Conform to the daily routine of the household. Be prompt at meals and helpful around the house. Keep your room in order and make your own bed. Adjust yourself in every possible way, and respond cheerfully to the efforts of your host to make your visit enjoyable.

Do not embarrass your host by refusing almost every dish that is served at the table. Take a little of everything, whether you like it or not.

Do not expect to be entertained all the time. Have a book to read or some other way of amusing yourself when your friend cannot be with you. Be considerate in your use of the radio or television. Let your host direct the choice of entertainment.

If your host takes you to a restaurant, order modestly. Do not order the most expensive item on the menu, or the least expensive (that would be too obvious). It is wisest to follow the lead of your host. Is he having appetizers or only the main course? Is anyone ordering dessert? A good host will ask whether you would like a first course or a dessert.

Moderate your use of the phone: long-distance calls, unless you use your own credit card, should be placed only in cases of urgent necessity, and with the permission of the host. Ask the operator for the charges so that you can reimburse your host.

When you have accepted hospitality, you are indebted to your host. If you cannot return it by entertaining in your own house, you can show your appreciation in many other ways, such as taking him to the theater or sending him a thoughtfully chosen gift.

If you have stayed overnight at a friend's house, within a week write a thank-you note in which you express your appreciation for the pleasant visit, but *never* write, "I hope that you can come to visit me soon so that I can return your kind hospitality."

There is no excuse for appearing on someone's doorstep without telephoning first to inquire whether your visit would be convenient. Even if a friend has invited you to stop by at any time, be sensitive to his mood and needs whenever you do, and take special care that you conclude your visit well before mealtime, so that you won't put your friend in the position of having to feed you.

You will avoid mistakes if you arrive in another country with some basic knowledge of the local customs and where they differ from your own. You can ask someone who has been there or study a guidebook of that country in the library or in a bookstore.

In deciding what to wear when you are a guest, you cannot go wrong by dressing more conservatively than you would at home. Once you have arrived, you will quickly notice what your friends are wearing. When in doubt, women should wear skirts (below the knee) rather than pants, and sleeves rather than tank tops. Avoid shorts and bare midriffs. Men should dress neatly, in shirts with sleeves and with the belt of their trousers at their waist.

At meals, observe your host and do as he does. If you are offered a dish of unknown ingredients, take at least a small serving; it might have been prepared as a special compliment to you and refusing it might offend your host. Notice also whether the other guests leave food on their plates when they are finished eating; in many countries, leaving a clean plate, as we are taught to do at home, means that you haven't had enough to eat and want more. Sometimes there isn't more, however, and the meal you just ate used up all the resources of the cook.

In some of the countries you visit, you may encounter families who still employ household help. You may be expected to leave them a small gift of money. Don't feel shy about asking your host what would be an appropriate amount. Hand it in an envelope directly to the person with your thanks, or leave it where it can be found when your room is cleaned after you leave.

The rules of courtesy you learn at home will serve you in good stead wherever you go. Sensitivity to those around you, an attitude of respect and acceptance of other customs, and a sincere friendliness will bridge most differences.

Manners maketh man.
—William of Wykeham (1324–1384)

IX

AT THE TABLE

❧

*A*lways cool, collected, and patient, the polite person dines slowly, deliberately, and with the air of someone who eats to live rather than lives to eat. The impolite person, on the contrary, is fidgety and nervous, eats fast, eagerly eyes the food as it appears, makes violent grabs at dishes as they are sent around, and uses his hands inappropriately.

The conversation at the table should always be pleasant, and of a kind in which all may take part. If you must say something disagreeable, wait until the meal is over, so that no one's appetite is spoiled. The pleasantest part of the meal should be the conversation.

Knowing the right thing to do is very different from being able to do it when the need arises. Good table manners come only from continual practice of the right way of doing things. Your own home is the right place to learn by observing good form at every meal.

DINING STYLES

There are two basic techniques for handling cutlery properly. One is American, the other is European. Although both are perfectly acceptable, the American style is less efficient and can appear clumsy. What is important is being consistent and correct in whichever style you choose.

In the American style, the knife is used for cutting only. Hold it in your right hand (if you are right-handed) while cutting, and the fork in your left hand, with the prongs down, to control the piece being cut. When you finish cutting the piece, put the knife down on the edge of the plate (blade facing in) and switch the fork to your right hand to lift the cut piece to your mouth. When not using the knife and fork, keep your hands in your lap.

In the European style, the knife remains in your right hand and the fork in your left, with its prongs downward when you lift the cut food to your mouth; you do not shift the fork back and forth every time you cut a piece of meat. To eat vegetables, use the fork with your right hand, prongs up, and place the knife on the plate, pointed in. The hands remain above the table from the wrist up when you are not using the knife and fork.

GENERAL TABLE PROTOCOL

Be prompt for meals. At the table, remain standing until all have arrived. It is customary for a man to help the lady on his left to be seated.

Never read at the table unless you are alone.

Never eat with your unused arm and elbow supporting your weight on the table as if you are so weak that you can barely lift the food to your mouth.

At a formal meal, food is served to you on your left side. Take the serving fork in your left hand and the serving spoon in your right. Take small portions. After you have served yourself, put the serving spoon and fork back side by side on the platter.

If you don't like what is served, it is permissible to refuse it discreetly. But don't be so obvious as to find yourself with an empty plate.

Do not start eating until all have been served, unless the host asks you to. If you are eating in a private home, remember that someone prepared the meal and compliment the cook.

If you must leave the table during the meal or before everyone else has finished, excuse yourself. Never use a cell phone at the table. If an emergency arises or business must be conducted, excuse yourself and leave the room. Telephone calls at meals are a nuisance and can be answered by the answering machine, which allows you to return calls at a more convenient time.

Pushing your plate away when you have finished is very rude.

Whether at a dinner party or a picnic, offer to help clean up. The offer is the important thing. Sometimes the host will not want you to help. If so, do not insist.

COURSES

Soup

When you are eating soup, hold the soupspoon in your right hand with the thumb on top. Sip the soup from the side of the spoon or from the end—it makes no difference. And please, no noise.

When you have finished eating the soup, place the spoon on the serving plate. Do not leave it on the soup plate.

Salad

You may use both the salad fork and knife for this course, leaving the knife on the table if it is not needed. At luncheon, salad is often served at the same time as the meat course. If so, you may use the same fork you are using for the meat.

If cheese is served with the salad, place a small portion of it on your salad plate along with crackers or bread. Use a salad knife to put the cheese on crackers or bread.

Round cheeses, like Brie or Camembert, are often presented in wedges like pie slices. When serving yourself, never take the "nose," or small end of the piece; cut off a smaller wedge along the side of the piece.

Fish

Both the fish knife and fork are used for the fish course. Prongs should *always* be down when the fork is held in the left hand.

Note that the fish knife is not held the same way the meat knife is held, but like a pencil. Holding the fork in your left hand, use the knife to cut and push the fish onto the fork.

If the fish is soft and boneless, then it is perfectly proper to use only the fish fork. When you are holding the fork in your right hand, the prongs may be up or down, whichever way is more convenient. When using only the fork, leave the knife on the table.

Meat

The meat knife is not held like the fish knife because cutting requires more leverage. Let your forefinger point down the handle. Never hold the fork in your left hand and pile food onto it with the knife.

If the meat does not require cutting, you may eat it with the fork in your right hand, leaving the knife on the table. When eating only with the fork, place it, *prongs up,* on the plate when you are finished.

Dessert

With the fork in your left hand, prongs down, eat the dessert with the spoon in your right hand. The fork here serves only as a pusher.

If dessert is a pie or a cake, only the fork need be used, and if it is ice cream or pudding, only the spoon. The other utensil is left on the table.

While eating dessert, put the fork and spoon into the same "rest" position you use for the knife and fork during the meat course. Place the fork prongs down, lying over the spoon.

To signal that you have finished eating dessert, place the fork and spoon side by side, bowl up, prongs up.

Coffee

In helping yourself to sugar, use the spoon provided, never your own. Be careful not to overload your cup with cream and sugar. Also avoid swirling your coffee around too energetically and splashing it into your saucer.

Don't slurp, but sip gently. If your coffee is too hot, let it sit for a while—don't blow on it.

Place your spoon on the saucer; don't leave it in the cup.

DINING PROTOCOL
Using Utensils

Most silverware is placed in the order of its use. Always start with the utensil of each type that is farthest from the plate. If you make a mistake, just continue eating. *Don't* put the silver back on the table. Be nonchalant.

When using the fork, rest it on your middle finger and guide it with your index finger and thumb, thumb on top. Please do not use it like a shovel.

In the simplest table setting, the knife is on the right of the plate, the fork on the left. The napkin is to the left of the fork. The soupspoon, next to the knife, is included only if soup is on the menu.

Be careful not to hold your knife and fork like weapons. It is perfectly proper to talk with the knife and fork in your hands, but do not wave around a fork or any other utensil, with or without food on it. The knife should *never* be raised more than an inch or two above the plate.

Cut food into small, bite-sized pieces, *one piece at a time.*

Once you have put food on a utensil, eat it. Do not hold it in midair while you talk or listen.

Never rest silverware on each side of your plate like oars dangling in the water. Once you pick up a piece of cutlery, it should not touch the table again. Knives rest on the plate, blade facing in and touching the inside of the plate. Only the handle should rest on the rim of the plate.

The only rest position is the knife and fork crossed on the plate with the fork over the knife, prongs down, as a sign that you are not finished.

When eating a piece of bread, drinking, talking, or wiping your mouth, place the knife and fork in the rest position. The sharp edge of the knife should be pointing to the left.

When you have finished the course, *always* place your knife and fork *side by side,* with the fork prongs pointing up and the blade of the knife facing the fork. This position signals that you are finished.

Napkins

Place your napkin on your lap only after the host has done so. Don't flap your napkin to unfold it. Keep it on your lap throughout the meal. If you leave the table, place your napkin to the left of your plate and push your chair back under the table.

A napkin should be used to dab the face, not wipe it. Before taking a drink, gently pat your mouth to remove any crumbs that have lingered there.

It goes without saying that you *never, under any circumstances,* use your napkin as a substitute handkerchief. If you burp, cover your mouth with your napkin and say, "Excuse me," to no one in particular.

Don't refold your napkin at the end of the meal. Pick it up from the center and place it loosely on the table beside your plate.

Chewing

Keep your lips closed while chewing your food. Don't put too much food in your mouth, and eat slowly. You are not tossing hay into your barn to beat the rain.

Do not slurp or make any other unattractive noises when eating. Never talk when your mouth is full. If someone addresses you when you have a full mouth, let the person wait for your answer until you have swallowed. If you eat slowly, taking small bites, you will seldom be caught at a disadvantage.

If you find some gristle or a piece of meat you cannot swallow, don't spit it onto your plate or into your fist. Chew it into as small a piece as possible and then place it on the prongs of your fork (or into your spoon if the course calls for a spoon). Put it on the rim of your plate. Don't be embarrassed—this placement is perfectly correct. Remove olive pits or fish bones with your fingers.

Passing Dishes

Begin by passing any serving dishes in front of you. Pass to your right. Never reach across the table or in front of someone to help yourself to a dish, but ask the person nearest you to pass it.

Try to anticipate the needs of your neighbors; offer them what they need before they have to ask. Always say "Please" and "Thank you" when foods are passed to you or when accepting or declining them.

Pass pitchers, creamers, and cutlery—anything with a handle—by turning the handle toward the person receiving it.

When passing salt and pepper, place the shakers on the table. Some people are superstitious and believe it is bad luck to have salt and pepper shakers handed to them. And, yes, the two should always be passed together even if only one has been requested.

Appearance

Young people, properly trained, are easy and natural in their bearing at the table. They never slump in their chair, and they do not annoy their neighbors by wiggling their legs or playing with their bread or any other object on the table.

Sit up straight. Keep your elbows off the table when eating (this is part of sitting up straight), although you may rest them on the table between courses or when you are not eating. Keep your elbows close to your sides, and do not throw your arm over the back of your chair or push your chair away from the table until everyone stands to leave.

Each time you take a mouthful, lean over your plate. If anything drops, it will fall on the plate and not on your clothes.

Breaking Bread

Put butter first on your bread plate or dinner plate, not directly on your roll. Always take bread with your fingers, never with your fork. Tear bread into bite-sized pieces and butter each piece just before you eat it, never the entire roll or slice of bread.

Food Stuck in Your Teeth

If food gets stuck in your teeth, it is quite unattractive to pick at it with your finger or a toothpick. Also unattractive is moving your tongue around in your mouth trying to dislodge it. If the food causes enough discomfort to need remedy, excuse yourself and go remove it in private.

Purses and Briefcases

Keep purses and briefcases off the table, as well as keys, hats, gloves, eyeglasses, cases, and cell phones. In short, if it isn't part of the meal, keep it off the table.

Seasoning

Don't salt or otherwise season your food before you taste it. To do so is particularly offensive when the cook is sitting at the table (usually during a meal in a private home).

Public Grooming

For anyone who needs to be told, applying makeup at the table is in the worst possible taste. The dining table is not a vanity, nor is it a hair salon. Guests who need to fix their hair or makeup are advised to retire to the nearest bathroom for such personal attention.

EATING CHALLENGES

~ *Artichokes:* Pull off the leaves one at a time and draw them through your teeth. When you get to the heart, use a knife to scrape off the fuzzy part, and then proceed with your fork and knife.

~ *Asparagus:* Eat asparagus with your fingers unless the stalks are too long. If the asparagus is long, limp, or thin, cut off the end with your fork held in your right hand and eat it with your fork. Then pick up the shortened stalk with your fingers.

~ *Bacon:* Eat bacon with your fingers if it is crisp. Otherwise, use a knife and fork.

~ *Cake:* You may eat cake with your fingers if it is bite-sized. If it's not, if it's sticky, or if it's served with sauce or ice cream, both the fork and spoon come into play. Hold the spoon in your right hand to scoop up the dessert. The fork goes in your left hand and is used as a pusher.

~ *Caviar:* Spread caviar on toast with a knife and eat it with your fingers.

~ *Celery, olives, pickles, and radishes:* These foods are eaten with your fingers as well.

~ *Chicken:* You may eat chicken with your fingers at picnics and informal family dinners. It is more polite to use a knife and fork on other occasions. Use your hostess as a guide. If she picks up the chicken and eats it with her fingers, you may too. If she does not eat it this way, stick with the fork and knife.

~ *Corn on the cob:* Use both hands to eat corn on the cob, even if you aren't on a picnic.

~ *Hard-shelled crab and lobster:* Shellfish requires a number of strategies. Crack the shell with a nutcracker and extract the meat with a three-tined seafood fork. If you pull out a large piece, cut it with a fork. Pull off the small claws, and draw the meat out of them as if they were straws.

Nowhere are your manners more on display than at the dinner table. And there are few aspects of social etiquette that worry people more—for the most part, unnecessarily. There is no reason in the world to be intimidated by the prospect of even the most formal dinner. It is all a matter of knowing the basic rules and, if at a loss, watching to see what the host does. Once learned, these rules become second nature and enable you to approach dining in public with confidence, to relax, to enjoy the meal and the company.

Dining with others can be one of life's most pleasant experiences. You can enjoy it more fully when you know what to expect and what is expected of you.

The greater man the greater courtesy.
—Alfred, Lord Tennyson (1809–1892)

X

CONDUCT IN PUBLIC PLACES

*Y*our conduct in public should be marked by quiet dignity. The keynote of good manners is unobtrusiveness.

When you are out in public, keep in mind three principles. The first is to treat everyone you meet with kindness. Your sensitivity toward those you meet may brighten their day.

The second is to take no one for granted. Be aware of the people around you and their rights to the public space you share. Don't simply ignore the waitress, the sales clerk, or the bus driver; be sincerely grateful for all services and thank those who provide them.

The third is to respect others. Be helpful to the elderly, the infirm, and the physically challenged. Tactfully offer assistance when you can, open doors for them, and always let them pass before you.

When in public, dress in a way that does not invite stares. Avoid brushing your hair or applying makeup in public.

These activities have a place, but that is not the bus, the train, or the sidewalk.

Here are certain situations that bear specific attention.

ON THE STREET

Keep your voice down and your stereo off when you are walking down the street; keep the volume low on the car radio if you are driving. Noise pollution has become a serious problem. Do not add to it by using your car horn, revving your motorcycle engine, or shouting into your cell phone.

Greet acquaintances with a nod or a smile. If you want to chat, don't stop in the middle of the sidewalk but walk with your friend to a place where you will not be in the way. Eating or chewing gum with your mouth open as you stroll along is very unattractive.

ON PUBLIC TRANSPORTATION

The same guidelines apply when you ride in a bus, a train, a plane, or a ferry. Talking or laughing loudly with your friends may seem harmless and reasonable to you, but in reality you are invading the space of the people around you and being annoying. Noise is amplified in enclosed spaces.

Give up your seat when an older person, a mother with a child, a pregnant woman, or a handicapped person enters the bus. Don't rush to get ahead of the others or push your way out.

IN A CAR

If you are a passenger in a car, ask permission to open or close windows and to regulate the heat, the air conditioning, or the radio. If you are the driver, be attentive to the needs of your passengers.

When driving a car, remember to give space to the other drivers and be patient. Even if you are in a hurry, remember that it is not only courteous to avoid tailgating, but safer. It is also safer to pull off the road when you need to call someone on the car cell phone.

Avoid taking up two parking spaces. When you are parallel parking, make sure that the cars in front and in back of you can get out easily.

It doesn't hurt to give in. If another driver's rudeness irritates you, do not show your anger or make any gestures. The other driver's manners will not improve if you do, and you may be putting yourself in danger if he chooses to retaliate.

IN THEATERS, MUSEUMS, AND CHURCHES

Attending the theater, art galleries, museums, and church services has its own requirements. It is very important to arrive early enough to be seated before the ceremony or performance begins. If you are late and it is at all possible, wait for the intermission (or proper interlude) to find your seat. Apologize for the interruption as you pass by those who are already seated.

During the program be quiet and attentive. It is very distracting to be seated near someone who is rattling his program, asking questions, or voicing his opinion about what is going on. When the program is over and you have applauded with everyone else, leave with the flow of people in your section. Do not rush out and climb over the people still in their seats.

IN RESTAURANTS, HOTELS, AND SHOPS

When you go to a restaurant, a hotel, a shop, or any other such place, keep your voice down and be pleasant to the people who serve you. Always address them respectfully and thank them for what they do. If a service provider does something special or extra, tell him how much you appreciate it. If you are at a restaurant or receive special services in a hotel, be sure to leave a tip (15 to 20 percent is customary); waiters rely on tips to supplement their wages.

It may happen that you are unhappy with the services rendered: the meal was not good, the service was too slow, the towels were missing, there was a large insect on your bed. Mention your dissatisfaction in a respectful tone of voice; often the problem is not the fault of the first person you see. You have probably heard someone in an airport yelling at one of the clerks because the plane is late. You may also have noticed that the clerk usually maintains amazing courtesy and self-control in spite of the irate customer's display of temper. Take the clerk's manner as a model, not the customer's.

Always keep in mind the simple concepts of respect for everyone and never taking anyone for granted. Remember to be true to yourself and have the courage of your convictions. Do not change who you are in order to fit in with the crowd by going along with things you know are wrong or unsuitable. Although this may sometimes be hard to do, you will earn the respect of your peers, and, more important, you will maintain your integrity and self-respect.

To be of no church is dangerous. Religion . . . will glide by degrees
out of the mind unless it be invigorated and reimpressed by . . .
stated calls to worship, and the salutary influence of example.
—*Samuel Johnson (1709–1784)*

XI

CONDUCT IN PLACES OF WORSHIP

꧁

𝓡espect is the guiding principle behind proper conduct in places of worship, whether of your own religious faith or someone else's.

As a member of your own faith, you have learned to respect its places of worship and its customs and rituals. When you visit an unfamiliar church, synagogue, temple, mosque, or shrine, always conduct yourself with consideration and respect for the members, as you would your own.

The question is to know what kind of behavior is appropriate for these places. Do you observe total silence? Are you expected to make a contribution, to join the congregation in song or at the altar, to remove your shoes, to cover or uncover your head?

The solution often depends on why you are there. If you are a guest attending a ceremony—a marriage, a confirmation, or a service to mark the death of a friend or a relative—you probably have available that great resource, the "native guide." Ask him how you should behave, what to wear, and what to expect. Also watch what others are doing. Even if you miss something, it will be clear to your friends and others that you are doing your best to respect their traditions.

When you travel to remote sites of art, worship, or antiquity, you may find yourself either on your own or in a herd of fellow travelers, some of whose behavior is as offensive to you as it is to the local population. (You hope no one will think that you are one of them!) Be alert for signs posted at the entrance of the buildings begging visitors not to litter, take photos, smoke, wear bathing suits, and so on. It is the behavior of some visitors that has forced those sites to put up such signs, in several languages. (American tourists are not the only ones who commit these offenses.)

Although religious systems differ in how they define appropriate dress, you would be wise to dress conservatively and modestly. Women should wear long sleeves, a skirt falling below the knee, and a scarf to protect the head; men should wear long-sleeved shirts and long pants. Men as well as women need to be aware that the standards of decency in other cultural settings often require that they cover up more than would be necessary at home. Conversely, in some places you may be expected to remove your shoes or your hat.

Be especially sensitive to the possibility that your camera can be offensive. Make sure that taking pictures is permitted inside a house of worship. The blinding flash, the grinding film advance, and the purring camcorder, into which the operator mutters his incessant commentary, are all potential stumbling blocks to smooth interfaith understanding.

When you are learning about a new place, at home or abroad, you may want to visit a house of worship during a service as a way of understanding the people who live there. But first you must find out whether visitors are permitted and what is expected of them. In some communities abroad, as well as in the United States, especially where people have been subjected to persecution or discrimination, strangers may not be welcomed into the heart of communal life. Visitors may be tolerated at services in your own religious tradition, even actively welcomed, but do not assume that this is true everywhere. Remember, during the many centuries when Christianity was a persecuted sect, only the baptized were allowed to attend the entire Mass!

Ask politely if you may attend a religious service, and do not take a refusal personally, but accept it as gracefully as possible. If admitted, put your camera away, be alert for cues, and be patient. If you are lucky, you will meet a local member who will take it upon himself to educate you.

CONDUCT IN A CATHOLIC CHURCH

Appropriate conduct in a Catholic church has changed since the great Vatican Council II of 1962–64. By opening many areas of practice in the Church to reexamination and renewal, Pope John XXIII expressed his desire "to let some fresh air in here." The solemnity and strict silence have given way to a freer atmosphere, and the faithful participate more actively in the celebration of the Mass.

Women, once relegated to supporting roles outside the sanctuary, now have joined the ranks of altar servers, lectors, and eucharistic ministers. The liturgical use of Latin has vanished from the majority of parishes.

Formerly, the Mass was seen as a setting for an individual to commune with God through the sacramental agency of the priest at the altar; there was no direct involvement with fellow parishioners. Now, although some Catholics still prefer this manner of worship, the American bishops endorse congregational participation as a valuable way to encourage the development of a true spiritual family. They remind the faithful that Christ is present equally in the Eucharist, the Scriptures, and the community of believers. Church members are expected to participate in and respond in unison to the prayers of the Mass, to greet one another ("Peace be with you") after the Consecration, and to hold each other's hands during the "Our Father." All of these changes have come in a period of less than forty years.

In church as elsewhere, respect for others requires that you try to avoid making your appearance and conduct a source of distress to other people. Be reserved in your dress and behavior. God may not care if you come to His house wearing tennis shorts, but some of the older members of the congregation will be scandalized. Many people now seem to think that it is all right to chat freely in church; you should not follow their example, because it disturbs those who want to meditate or concentrate on their prayers and on the ceremony. Conversation in the vestibule is fine, but keep your voice low enough so that it will not carry into the church.

When you enter a Catholic church, make the sign of the cross with fingers that have been dipped in the holy water fount, and wait for the usher, if there is one, to indicate where you should sit. Genuflect, kneeling briefly on one knee, before you enter the pew and before you leave. Take your place quietly, nodding politely to your neighbors.

When the altar servers enter the church leading the procession of lector, eucharistic ministers, and priest, you should stand and join in singing the entrance hymn. (If you cannot carry a tune, you may remain mercifully silent.) For standing, sitting, or kneeling, follow the practice of the congregation. Whatever the accepted mode in a particular parish, you will notice a few recalcitrant folk who prefer to kneel throughout the service. Be sensitive to their preferences. If you are seated in front of someone who is kneeling, do not settle back against your seat but give him a little space. When approaching the altar to receive communion, follow the pattern adopted by the congregation.

Do not bolt from the church after a service. Wait until the celebrant has left the altar and gone out of the church before leaving your place.

Whether you are adapting to other customs as a guest, a traveler-tourist, or an observer of community life, you will find, as others have, that the exercise of restraint and sensitivity will reward you not only with a new appreciation of other religious traditions but also with a stronger appreciation and greater respect for your own.

A good conscience is a continual feast.
—*Robert Burton (1577–1640)*

XII

CONDUCT IN SCHOOL

⬥

*Y*our courtesy is real only if your good manners are a true expression of your inner self. This is what integrity is all about. Everyone you meet and associate with will recognize this inner quality of sincerity and truth, just as phoniness is also easily recognizable. When you focus on others, you feel less shy and self-conscious.

When you greet your fellow students during free time, walking to and from class, your friendly acknowledgment should be based on a sincere attitude of friendliness. You don't have to think of this each time you encounter someone, but if integrity and concern for others are intrinsic to your character, your external behavior will be a natural expression of your inner self.

What if there is someone you can't stand? You don't have to become this person's best friend, but when you run into him or her, behave as you would toward anyone else.

Be conscious of the people around you, acknowledge them with a smile, and include them in your conversation.

Whenever people are talking together, walk *around* them, not *through* them. If you need to speak to a member of the group, do not interrupt but wait quietly. Of course, if some of your friends are talking in a group, you can feel free to join in.

When you are in a group, make sure to welcome a new-comer, make him feel comfortable with a greeting, and catch him up with whatever subject you are discussing.

If you notice someone who is always alone in the hall or in the lunchroom, make a special effort to talk to that person and to include him in some of your activities. You may discover a new friend.

Treat teachers, students, and visitors with the same amount of respect. "Please" and "Thank you" have a greater value than the small effort they require. Don't ignore your teachers when you see them outside the classroom. Open and close the door for them and let them walk in ahead of you; if a teacher is carrying a heavy load, offer to help. When visitors are on campus, graciously go out of your way to help them find the place or person they are looking for or to answer their questions.

Out of respect for your teachers and classmates, be on time for class. Be prepared with the necessary supplies; come in and sit down, ready to work.

Participate thoughtfully in class discussion, but do not monopolize it. When you know the answers and like to talk, it is easy to monopolize the discussion quite unintentionally.

Some students try to distract the teacher by asking improper questions, or they bait the teacher to get a reaction. They may do this to attract attention or to entertain their classmates. This immature behavior is rude, unkind, and interruptive.

If you have a problem with a teacher, ask to speak to him privately at a designated time when you can express your problem or frustration without causing a public scene. You will discover how concerned and supportive your teacher can be.

When you are working or studying in class, do not disturb those around you. Keep your desk and the floor around you in order so that a teacher or classmate moving around the room does not trip over your backpack or books. Also, in case of an emergency, everyone needs a clear path to the door.

When you turn in an assignment, it is very important that the work be truly yours. This may seem obvious, but it is extremely easy to copy, even without realizing it, because the resources are so readily available. Any phrase or group of words that is "borrowed" from a resource is plagiarized if it is not properly noted. An honest student would never turn in plagiarized work, just as he would never copy homework from another student or cheat on a test.

The purpose of an assignment is to train you in writing and research. If you copy work, you are not gaining the knowledge you need for future success and your dishonesty damages your integrity. George Washington, at age fourteen, wrote this exhortation in his "Rules of Civility": "Labor to keep alive in your breast that little celestial fire called conscience."

Keep in mind the time and effort your teachers give to your education. Don't forget to say "Good-bye" and "Thank you" to them when you leave at the end of a term or before a vacation. If your parents are on campus, make sure they meet your teachers. Parents are your staunchest backers and supporters. Give them the opportunity to share in your progress.

Thank the teacher and staff members when they have gone out of their way for you, whether a teacher has given you extra help on an assignment or a custodian has opened your locker for you. You can show your gratitude on special occasions, such as Christmas, at the end of the year, or at graduation by sending a note of thanks, which is always greatly appreciated.

In school as elsewhere, courtesy boils down to the simple precept of treating others as you would like them to treat you.

The greatness of work is inside the individual.
—*Pope John Paul II (1920–)*

XIII

CONDUCT IN THE WORKPLACE

❧

At work, practice your daily code of conduct as you would anywhere else: treat every person with whom you come in contact with courtesy whether they be clients, customers, or fellow workers.

THE RÉSUMÉ

Unless you are skilled in résumé preparation, you would be well advised to seek the services of a professional résumé writer. Throughout your career your résumé should be periodically updated with your working history, but if you have just graduated and are entering the business world for the first time, your educational background should be extensively detailed. The résumé of the young applicant should be filled with accomplishments—not only how much you did but how well you did it. If you achieved a high grade point average, include it in your résumé. Include also any organizations in which you were involved and through which you may have received recognition. Include awards or competitions you won as well as any activities or committees you led, assisted with, or excelled at. Recruiters want to see qualities of leadership.

THE SEARCH

Today you can search for a job in a multitude of ways. All major newspapers have web sites, as do consortia of major companies. Research a company's stock information, history, and financial background and decide whether you want to send in your résumé. Present a résumé that is not too long but full of accomplishments.

You can also use employment services, but don't rely only on them. They fall usually into two categories: search firms to which the job searcher pays a fee and so-called head-hunter firms that are hired by employers to find employees.

Often a friend or co-worker knows of a job opening. Most colleges and graduate schools have job banks. Your public library can lead you to online or community resources, and don't overlook the want ads in the *Wall Street Journal,* trade magazines, or your local newspaper.

Professionals now commonly form groups to keep up with developments in their field. They exchange leads and make contacts in their area of expertise. Try to seek out organizations in the fields that interest you. It is a very efficient way to find positions that may never be advertised.

THE INTERVIEW

Remember that you are selling yourself to a prospective employer. Your dress should be appropriate and your jewelry understated. Give yourself time to prepare, both at home and on the way to your interview. Stay calm. Arrive five minutes early or *exactly* on time. Announce yourself to the receptionist but *do not engage in conversation*. Take a seat (preferably in a straight-back chair, not the cozy sofa). If there is paperwork to be filled out, return it promptly after completing it. Do not stand or walk about the reception area looking at artwork, citations, or diplomas on the walls. Go back to the chair, sit without slouching, and try to relax.

Impeccable credentials are commendable, but the first impression counts the most. Visual poise, the persona of a professional, and being sincere cannot be stressed enough. From your entrance, your firm handshake, and your direct eye contact, the interviewer is acutely aware of your entire demeanor.

Ask intelligent questions about training and opportunities for advancement. It is not uncommon for an interview to be conducted before a panel of interviewers with one person facilitating the questioning. Do not be (or appear to be) intimidated by the panel, but think before you speak. Be brief and to the point with your answers. Often you will be asked a psychological question. Its purpose is to see how well you handle yourself under pressure. A panel interview always includes a question so broad that it cannot be intelligently answered: for example, "So, Miss Jones, how do you like living in America?" When you are asked such a question, do not be afraid to use humor in your response. Humor is a welcome quality in the workplace.

When the interview is over, do not make a hasty retreat, but stand and thank the panel for its time. If you can handle the panel interview and maintain a level of self-assurance, you are more likely to be remembered and chosen over someone with comparable credentials who was mentally unprepared or intimidated by the group. Whether you have a single or a group interview, follow up immediately with a brief thank-you note to each person expressing your appreciation for his time and kindness.

THE WORKPLACE

What you wear has a subliminal effect. Dressing conservatively in properly fitted clothes in basic colors (black, navy, gray, or beige) and classic styles is preferable to showing off the latest fashion trend. Once employed, many young people make the mistake of "retiring" their "interview outfit" and arriving at work in whatever suits their fancy. If they announce that "This is the real me!" their claim may be construed as evidence of having fraudulently represented themselves when applying for the position. Any such change in the business-like look adopted for the interview results in a confusing persona and is not compatible with success in the workplace.

If you occupy a management position, you do not want to look less than serious. It is unfortunate that some people today have conflicting ideas about their wardrobe and its coordination. As a result, companies have issued dress codes defining what is appropriate and inappropriate attire. The dress code is not a list of suggestions but a mandate to which employees are expected to adhere. Infractions could show up in your periodic review.

Of course, not all places of employment are the same and your working attire depends on your environment. For example, professions in the arts sanction creativity in dress and accept the dramatic and exotic. Although you should avoid wearing oversized jewelry in any workplace (earrings should never be long and dangling), you can still be fashionable. The impression you want to achieve is a no-nonsense, no-frills, professional look.

Once you complete your job assignment, it may be worth your while to familiarize yourself with all departments to see how your company works as a whole. Memorize the names and titles of department heads; when you can "put the face with the name," be cordial and *use the name* if you happen to pass a person you recognize in a hallway or elevator. You will be remembered positively for doing so in a pleasant manner.

Always return promptly from your lunch hour and breaks even if your superiors or colleagues do not.

Be willing to work extra hours on special assignments or emergencies, but do not make it a habit, for overtime work will become expected and unappreciated. Be helpful whenever and however you can, but make sure that the work falls under your job description.

Do not boast of your past experiences or give everyone a verbal résumé of your background or your education. Your superiors are aware of your qualifications; otherwise, they would not have hired you. Your co-workers will soon learn your value from your good work.

Never discuss salary, either yours or a colleague's, with anyone, with the exception of your direct supervisor or the human resources department. Don't ask and don't tell!

If you are harassed in any way—by consistent innuendos, lewd or suggestive comments, an inappropriate touch, or any comments of a sexual nature—you must report it immediately to the human resources department and keep it strictly confidential.

Do not gossip or engage in any conversation about another employee. If you find yourself in the midst of such talk, excuse yourself and move to another location. Never grumble to another employee about a superior.

Many well-qualified, well-educated, and highly productive employees are terminated because of "poor attitude"—that is, for some of the offenses cited here. If you want to advance in a job, don't find fault with fellow employees or with company policy. Try always to interact harmoniously with everyone.

Hard work, a pleasant manner, integrity, competence, and common courtesy will work wonders.

We have decided to call the entire field . . . of communication theory, . . .
by the name of Cybernetics, which we form
from the Greek [for] steersman.
—Norbert Wiener (1894–1964)

XIV

ELECTRONIC COMMUNICATIONS

❧

General rules of courtesy apply to the use of our increasingly complex and varied means of communication. Above all, respect the time and privacy of others. Keep in mind certain rules that will help you choose the appropriate technology for each situation.

~ Written notes are still required when you are expressing sympathy for a loss, answering a formal invitation, or sending personal thanks or personal thoughts.

~ Use the telephone to convey news, announcements, congratulations, informal invitations and to keep in touch with family and friends.

~ The fax and e-mail are useful for urgent announcements, messages too long for the telephone, business and political letters, lists, clippings, pictures, and certain documents. E-mail to friends and relatives who live far away can make up for time differences that make it difficult to find them at home or awake. E-mail also costs less than telephone calls.

THE TELEPHONE

However useful it is, the telephone can be an intrusion that calls for consideration and judgment. Be considerate about the time of your call and its length. Ask yourself, "Does this person need to hear this? Right now? Is the telephone the best way to communicate my message?" Ask the answering party, "Is this a good time to call?" and do not go on for too long.

Be cordial when calling or answering. Speak clearly and always identify yourself. When you call a friend and his mother answers, always say, "Hello, Mrs. Behr, this is Kim Jones. May I speak to Kevin?" A parent, a friend, or a roommate is not a switchboard operator.

Know what you want to say before calling and do not interrupt the call for other things. Call waiting, for example, can be an annoying interruption. You can alleviate that either by having a message center that records your calls when you are on the line or by asking the first caller to hold for a moment, then picking up the second call and asking for a number where you can call right back. If the second call is more urgent than the first, ask the caller to hold; return to the first caller and explain that you need to take the second call but will call back as soon as you are done. The key is to show consideration to each caller and to return calls as soon as you can.

When answering the call for someone else, be sure the caller knows that you are not the person he was calling. Take and deliver any messages conscientiously.

THE CELLULAR PHONE

The cell phone should be used in public only for emergencies when other means are not available and for brief calls to apologize for running late.

It is extremely rude and inconsiderate to take private or business calls at social meetings or any place where the sounds may be disruptive. For example, you can use a cell phone in a drugstore while waiting for a prescription to be filled, as long as you keep your voice low. Do not use it in a restaurant where you are sitting with a friend. To avoid being a nuisance to others, turn off your cell phone or set its ring very low before entering a church, a theater, or a restaurant. At the very least, excuse yourself and take the call in the restroom, the lobby, or near a public phone. The same rules apply to the use of beepers.

Using a cellular phone while driving a car is dangerous and is best avoided. A 1997 study published in the *New England Journal of Medicine* found that a driver talking on a phone is four times more likely to be in an accident and that talking on a phone in a car is as dangerous as driving under the influence of alcohol.

Calls to cell phones should be kept to a minimum because of the interruption and the cost to both parties.

THE ANSWERING MACHINE

The answering machine is a way to communicate without inconveniencing the other person. If your message is long, ask for a return call and specify times when you can be reached or consider using the fax or e-mail. When you leave a message on an answering machine, speak clearly and slowly and, if necessary, leave your name and number. Because of the lack of privacy, do not leave messages of a personal nature.

The outgoing answering machine message should be short and clear. Subjecting callers to a five-minute program of "witticisms" or children's babble may not be as amusing to others as it is to you, particularly if the call is long-distance or related to business. The person receiving the message should answer as soon as possible, within twenty-four hours.

THE FAX MACHINE

When sending an important fax for business or personal reasons, you may want to call beforehand to see whether it is a convenient time to receive a fax, and afterward to find out whether it arrived. If you have more than ten pages to fax, use the mail. Confidential messages should be delivered face-to-face or by mail.

E-MAIL

Sending e-mail requires the same attention to the basic rules of English grammar as does letter writing. Because it is such a quick way to communicate, many people tend not to think before writing and to let inaccuracies stand. Edit your letters and use short paragraphs with indentations and spacing between them. Even though e-mail is less intrusive than the telephone, you should still be concise and to the point.

Be aware that e-mail is not always secure from prying eyes, especially if sent over an office network. Also remember that when you use e-mail—or go online for any other reason—you are tying up the phone line unless there is more than one. Make sure that your use of the Internet does not inconvenience others in the household.

Don't send e-mail attachments unless they are short or necessary. If you are thinking about sending a large photo of your puppy's latest exploit, be aware that it takes the recipient a long time to download the image. Don't send jokes or chain e-mails before asking the recipient whether this is acceptable.

Be sure to check your e-mail regularly so that you can return your messages promptly. It is frustrating to senders to be left in the dark as to why you haven't responded.

When using a chat room, be polite and friendly but circumspect. Confidential and private matters are not appropriate subjects for the Internet, nor is referring to a private individual by name.

Always keep in mind how important it is to maintain a healthy balance between the time you spend on your computer and the time you spend with your friends. Norman Nie, a political scientist at Stanford University, observes that "when you spend your time on the Internet, you don't hear a human voice and you never get a hug."

There are three lessons I would write,
Three words as with a burning pen,
In tracings of eternal light
Upon the hearts of men.
Hope, faith, and love.
—Johann Christoph Friedrich von Schiller (1759–1805)

XV

STATIONERY ETIQUETTE

Writing letters is something more than putting one word after another upon paper. It is an art. Directness, frank sincerity, regard for the interests and feelings of others, a certain insight into human nature, and a knowledge of form are all required to write a good letter.

Today letter writing is something of a lost art. In our hurried lives the e-mail, telephone calls, and answering machine messages have nearly replaced the well-written correspondence of our grandparents.

But there are still letters that should be handwritten: letters of condolence, congratulations, or introduction and thank-you notes for invitations and gifts.

The letter you write reflects your taste, your character, and your concern for how you present yourself. A sloppy letter that is badly worded, full of spelling errors, and written on unmatched paper and envelope will not make a very good impression.

Communications on paper are either informal, formal, or business-related. The most personal, of course, is the handwritten note or letter. Write neatly and legibly, try to write on a straight line, and keep an even margin. Don't send pages of writing that slides uphill and down in uncontrolled disorder.

Informal communications include informal invitations and greeting cards. You may write them by hand or create them on the computer. Other options are purchasing printed invitations that you fill in or ordering invitations from a catalog to be professionally printed.

Formal invitations are most commonly used for weddings, special celebrations, or large events sponsored by clubs or organizations. Their format includes text centered on the page, formal wording, and heavy paper. They are usually ordered through a printing company and can be engraved (for the most formal events) or printed.

Business letters and envelopes follow accepted standards of the working world. They must be typewritten or printed out from a computer file.

WRITING THE LETTER

Usually the date is placed at the upper right-hand side of the first page of a letter if the letter is not printed with an address or a monogram. If there is a printed address or mono-gram, the date may be placed on the lower left-hand side.

The salutation appears on the left side of the letter, fol-lowed by the body of the letter, then the closing and signa-ture on the right side. Please note, however, that many letter writers place the signature on the lower left side, followed by the address and date, if they are using stationery that is not printed with an address or monogram.

SOME COMPLIMENTARY CLOSINGS

Business	*Social Notes*	*Family and Friends*
Yours truly	Yours sincerely	Fondly
Yours very truly	Yours cordially	Affectionately
Yours respectfully	Gratefully yours	Love
Yours very sincerely	Affectionately yours	Lovingly
Sincerely yours	Regretfully	
Yours cordially		
Sincerely		
Cordially		

TEXT AND CONTENT

Be brief, accurate, clear, courteous, and sincere.

Make sure the words are spelled correctly, especially proper names. Avoid underscoring, exclamation points, and postscripts.

If you need to apologize for a belated reply, do so in the body or conclusion of your letter, not at the start.

Avoid using abbreviations, symbols, or initials for some-one's name. Use February for Feb., Street for St., number for #, and so forth.

STYLE

~ Choose an appropriate size of stationery to fit your mes-sage and a correct style for the occasion. Never use pre-lined paper or paper unmatched to the envelope.

~ When sending a handwritten letter, write or print legi-bly, on a straight line, and with an even margin. Use a pen, *not* a pencil.

~ Nicknames may be acceptable in *casual* correspondence ("Binkie" Ellis), but in formal communications use for-mal names (Barbara Ellis).

Make it a rule to reread every letter before you seal and mail it. If this rule were universal, many letters would never be sent and others would be rewritten.

STATIONERY

Do not write on both sides of semitransparent paper.

Insert the message into the envelope so that its recipient can remove it from the flap side of the envelope in the most readable direction.

If you feel overwhelmed with choices and are unsure what

stationery to choose, take a trip to your neighborhood quality stationery store. Look through the store's stock and catalogs for paper, style, fonts, and samples of personalization using initials, monograms, or address imprinting. A knowledgeable salesperson can help you make the right decision for the right usage.

PERSONALIZATION

Men or women can use their name alone, or their three initials without their address, at the top of stationery sheets or note cards. Initials are printed in the same size and match the first name, middle name, and surname, in that order. John Robert Dubin's initials would be J.R.D.

When using a monogram, make the surname initial the largest and put it in the center.

~ Anne Marie Bianco (single) would read A B M

~ Anne Bianco Young (married) would read A Y B

~ Anne and Robert Young (married) would read A Y R

NAMES AND TITLES

~ Never start a letter with "Dear Madam" or "Dear Sir." The recipient has a name.

~ A young boy can be addressed as "Master" to about the age of six. Then he uses just his given name until he has completed high school. After high school, young men are addressed as "Mr."

~ Professional men and women use "Mr.," "Dr.," etc., or simply their *full* name followed by their professional title: James Herrera, M.D., Director; Sarah B. Moore, Esq.

~ A girl is addressed as "Miss" from birth. Women may be addressed as "Ms." socially and professionally or with their full name, followed by their title.

~ A married or widowed woman is addressed socially using her husband's name: "Mrs. Robert Reich." She can also drop the Mrs. and add her maiden name to her husband's name: "Elizabeth Doyle Reich." This is a wise choice for signing legal documents.

~ A divorced woman has many choices. The simplest is to replace her former husband's name with her own: "Mrs. Elizabeth Doyle." She can also resume her maiden name using "Ms."

When in doubt, observe how someone signs his or her name and, if possible, ask their preference.

Addressing Envelopes

Social correspondence, including printed informal invitations, should always be addressed by hand in ink. The return address looks best on the envelope's back flap.

Formal invitations should also always be addressed by hand in ink. The return address should be printed, embossed, or written on the back flap of the envelope.

Business envelopes are addressed to match the heading of the letter. The return address is on the upper left-hand corner. Computer labels or word processor addresses are acceptable for business letters, but *please* never use this short-cut for social notes, Christmas cards, or announcements.

The postage stamp should be carefully placed on the upper right-hand corner of the envelope. The stamp that teeters at an angle spoils the look of the envelope.

To ensure prompt delivery of your correspondence, use correct zip codes and the two-letter state abbreviations provided by the U.S. Post Office.

Alabama	AL	Hawaii	HI
Alaska	AK	Idaho	ID
Arizona	AZ	Illinois	IL
Arkansas	AR	Indiana	IN
California	CA	Iowa	IA
Colorado	CO	Kansas	KS
Connecticut	CT	Kentucky	KY
Delaware	DE	Louisiana	LA
District of Columbia	DC	Maine	ME
Florida	FL	Maryland	MD
Georgia	GA	Massachusetts	MA

Michigan	MI	Oregon	OR
Minnesota	MN	Pennsylvania	PA
Mississippi	MS	Rhode Island	RI
Missouri	MO	South Carolina	SC
Montana	MT	South Dakota	SD
Nebraska	NE	Tennessee	TN
Nevada	NV	Texas	TX
New Hampshire	NH	Utah	UT
New Jersey	NJ	Vermont	VT
New Mexico	NM	Virginia	VA
New York	NY	Washington	WA
North Carolina	NC	West Virginia	WV
North Dakota	ND	Wisconsin	WI
Ohio	OH	Wyoming	WY
Oklahoma	OK		

When you are sending a letter out of the United States, be sure to include the name of the country and any postal code. Otherwise, you run the risk that your letter to Paris, France, will end up in Paris, Texas.

She'll wish there was more, and that's the great art o' letter writing.
—*Charles Dickens (1812–1870)*

XVI

PERSONAL CORRESPONDENCE

෴

The handwritten note or letter is best for messages of thanks, congratulations, introduction, or condolence. Informal invitations and replies, which also may be handwritten, are discussed in chapter XVII. Notes in printed greeting cards sent for holidays and special occasions are more appreciated by family and friends when written by hand rather than by computer. All correspondence should be place in the envelope in the position to be read most easily when the recipient removes it from the envelope.

Appropriate choices of stationery include

~ *Single heavy card stock:* Insert into the envelope face up.

~ *Informal notepaper, pre-folded at the top:* Additional text may be written inside. If the notepaper has a picture or imprint on the front, insert into the envelope face up. If the notepaper is pre-folded at the left edge, insert into the envelope fold-side down.

~ *Small letter paper sheet:* Text appears on page front. Fold in half, text inside. Insert into the envelope, fold-edge down.

~ *Larger letter paper sheet:* Use for longer letters or business correspondence. Fold in thirds, text inside. Insert into the envelope so that the second fold is at the bottom of the envelope.

THANK-YOU NOTES AND LETTERS

Always send a thank-you note within one week after receiving a gift, being entertained at a meal or as a house-guest, or receiving any other special invitation or favor.

Do not overlook immediate family members; if you have stayed at your grandparents' or cousin's house for a week, they deserve a written thank-you note.

A phone call is better than nothing, but since you should thank both your host and hostess, the phone can sometimes be awkward. A written note is easier.

Avoid using printed thank-you notepaper.

Here are three examples of thank-you messages for different circumstances. In the first, address the envelope to Mr. and Mrs. *Harold* Spring.

(date)

Dear Aunt Jane and Uncle Harry,

Thank you for your wonderful birthday gift. I love the two silver bangle bracelets and am enjoying wearing them. What a perfect remembrance of my sixteenth birthday!

I am looking forward to your next visit and hope you are both well.

Love,

(signature)

In the second example, the envelope should be addressed to Mr. (first name) Loar's home or office.

(date)

Dear Mr. Loar,

Thank you for the special tour of your office and for treating me to lunch. I appreciate the gift of your time and the opportunity to see a law office at work.

Mother and Dad add their warm regards to mine.

Yours sincerely,

(signature)

The third example is the bread-and-butter note written after you have been a houseguest. Address the envelope to the hostess only (Mrs. *Charles* Mendell). However, mention the host's name and any other family members in the text of the letter.

(date)

Dear Mrs. Mendell,

 My visit to you will always be one of my happiest memories. I enjoyed every moment of the week I spent with you.

 Best love to Mary and my kind regards to Dr. Mendell. Thank you all.

    Fondly,
    (signature)

LETTERS OF CONGRATULATION

The letter of congratulations should be natural and sincere. Two examples follow.

(date)

Dear John,

 Congratulations! I heard from your parents that you won the scholarship. All best wishes for a bright future filled with many great opportunities.

    Sincerely,
    (signature)

This note of congratulations could be written from one couple to another:

(date)

Dear Lenora and Edward,

Jim and I send all best wishes for your third anniversary. I will always treasure my memories of your wedding. Happiness always.

Love,

Betty (not Jim and Betty)

LETTERS OF CONDOLENCE

Condolence letters express our sympathy for the family and friends who have suffered a loss or the death of someone close. Send a few simple words as soon as you receive the news, either to the family member you know best or to the family member closest to the deceased.

All condolences should eventually be acknowledged by the recipient in the form of a personal note or by a relative or friend in the form of a pre-printed acknowledgment. Two examples of such exchanges follow:

(date)

Dear Agnes,

I have just read the announcement of your dear mother's death, and I send my sympathy and prayers to you. Your mother was a very special friend to me, and I shall always miss her.

Sincerely,
Ruth Lowe

(date)

Dear Mrs. Lowe,

I am grateful for your loving sympathy; your words were a great comfort to me and my family. Thank you for your many kindnesses to Mother during her lifetime.

Sincerely,
Agnes Jones

(date)

Dear Mary and Michael,

Please know our loving sympathy is with you. Jim and I are there for you whenever you need us. You are both in our thoughts and prayers.

Fondly,
Jane

(date)

Dear Jane and Jim,

Your words of sympathy and your prayers are greatly appreciated by me and Michael. We are very grateful for your thoughtfulness.

Fondly,
Mary

Here is an example of a pre-printed acknowledgment of a note of condolence:

The family of
(full name)
deeply appreciates
your kind expression
of sympathy

LETTERS OF INTRODUCTION

Letters of introduction should not be written indiscriminately. Write such letters only when there may be some benefit to *both* persons concerned, when you sincerely believe the two parties would enjoy knowing one another, and when the "host" person is a good friend, not a mere casual acquaintance.

Never ask for a letter of introduction. If your friend thinks a letter would help you, he will offer to send one without your asking.

All letters of introduction are written in a social form and addressed to the person to whom you are introducing your friend. Matters of a personal or private nature should not be included.

THE STANDARD BUSINESS LETTER

Always typewritten, business letters are as brief and explicit as possible. Business stationery consists of sheets of 8½-by-11 paper folded in thirds into a standard long envelope.

The basic elements of a business letter are

~ *Letterhead:* your name, address, and business telephone number at the top or bottom of the sheet (your personal telephone number, fax number, or e-mail address is optional)

~ *Date*

~ *Inside address:* the name and address of the person and firm to whom you are writing

~ *Salutation*

~ *Message*

~ *Complimentary closing*

~ Space for your *signature*

~ Your *name*

Two examples of business letters follow:

Beverly Jensen
349 Third Avenue
San Francisco, CA 94118

January 15, 1999

Mrs. Richard Green, Registrar
College of Alameda
250 College Avenue
Berkeley, CA 94110

Dear Mrs. Green:
Will you please send the latest college catalog to me at the following address:

Beverly Jensen
809 Union Street
San Francisco, CA 94113

Enclosed you will find a check in the amount of twenty dollars in payment for the catalog, including shipping costs.
Thank you for your prompt attention to this matter.
Yours truly,
Beverly Jensen

Sally Bryant
183 Downey Street
San Francisco, CA 94117

August 28, 1999

Mr. Richard S. Lopez
General Micro Systems
213 Fourth Street
San Francisco, CA 94104

Dear Mr. Lopez:

Margaret Murphy, of your company, suggested that I send you the enclosed résumé in reference to your search for a management trainee.

Earlier this year I graduated in the top 20 percent of my class at Ohio State University. My combined majors were business management and comparative literature.

During my junior and senior years I worked part-time in the supply department, assisting the director. Three months into my junior year he promoted me to oversee six students in the job of placing, organizing, and following up on orders for books, materials, furnishings, and janitorial supplies.

When I graduated, the director wrote a letter thanking me for a job well done and for my "energy, organization, and punctuality."

I spent several years in Europe while my father was stationed there with the U.S. Air Force. I am fluent in German and Spanish and know some French. My experience and interests would help me adapt quickly to this job.

I will call you the week of September 11 to arrange a suitable time to meet with you at your convenience.

Yours truly,

Sally Bryant

See ye not, courtesy
Is the true alchemy,
Turning to gold all it touches and tries?
—George Meredith (1828–1909)

XVII

INVITATIONS AND RESPONSES

❧

*A*n invitation, no matter how informal, should always be acknowledged within a week of its receipt. The answer must be a definite acceptance or regret, and you must abide by your decision one way or the other.

Whether formal or informal, written or printed, issued to a few or a multitude, an invitation needs to inform its recipient of the who, what, why, when, and where of an event.

Responses should be mirror images of the invitation. How you reply depends on the style of the invitation and the directives stated in it. The abbreviation RSVP stands for the French words "Répondez s'il vous plaît" and means "Please respond."

An invitation to stay at your house must state the dates of the start and end of the visit. In response, your guest needs to confirm the dates and times he plans to arrive and depart.

Using the Telephone for Invitations

Although the telephone is a quick way to issue informal invitations, it may be inefficient when inviting several people. There is also the risk that you may not say exactly the same thing to each guest or that someone may write down incorrect information about your event. You may use the telephone, however, as a supplement to your written invitation or in responses under some circumstances.

You may call prospective guests to say, "Please save this date for (the event). An invitation will be mailed shortly." The advantage of calling ahead is that you can obtain an approximate head count.

You may use your telephone to reply to an invitation when a phone number is indicated on it. *Never* e-mail or fax a reply to a social invitation.

Should illness or a crisis prevent you from attending an event, telephone your hostess immediately.

Informal Invitations and Replies

For a dinner, a handwritten invitation should be mailed three weeks ahead.

Dear Mrs. Arnold,

I am planning a small dinner party for my parents on Monday, March twenty-ninth, at seven o'clock. I hope you and Mr. Arnold will be able to attend. We are looking forward to seeing you.

Very cordially yours,
Katherine Wilson

March 6, 2000

The reply is addressed to Mrs. Robert Wilson only. If an acceptance, it reads:

Dear Katherine,

Mr. Arnold and I will be very happy to join you for dinner on March twenty-ninth at seven o'clock.

We look forward to seeing you, Bob, and your parents.

Sincerely,
Harriet Arnold

March 14, 2000

If a regret, the reply reads:

Dear Katherine,

We regret that we cannot accept your kind invitation for dinner on March twenty-ninth. Mr. Arnold and I will be on a trip.

We are so sorry to miss being with everyone. Warmest regards to you, Bob, and your parents.

Sincerely,

Harriet Arnold

March 14, 2000

There are limitless possibilities for creating your own informal invitations. For example, after drafting the text of the invitation and choosing a typeface, you could print out copies of it on high-quality pre-designed laser paper with matching envelopes.

If you choose to send fill-in informal invitations, visit a specialty stationery store, which will carry many different designs. Choose one that fits your party theme and fill in the blanks.

The most elegant fill-in invitation is printed on heavy card stock with simple engraved key words. In the following example, the words in parentheses were chosen by the sender to complete the invitation.

(Elizabeth Smith)
requests the pleasure of the company of
(Andrea Jones)
at *(a Graduation Tea for the Class of 2000)*
on *(Saturday, May sixth)*
at *(four o'clock)*
RSVP   *(790 Pine Road)*
(415–750–0973)   *(San Rafael)*

The same informal invitation ordered from a printer would look like this:

Elizabeth Smith
cordially invites you to
a Graduation Tea
in honor of the Class of 2000
on Saturday, May sixth
from four to six o'clock
at 790 Pine Road
San Rafael

Please reply
415–750–0973

FORMAL INVITATIONS AND REPLIES

Formal invitations are the most traditional. They are always ordered from a printing company or the stationery store. They may be printed on heavy card stock or on the formal "rag" paper folded on the left edge to resemble a two-page book.

The text appears on the front page only and is written in the third person. Phrasing is formal, date and numerals are spelled out, and no abbreviations are used. Formal invitations are mailed four to six weeks ahead of the event.

The reply, which should be prompt, is written on plain card stock or plain formal book-fold paper unless a printed reply card and envelope are provided with the invitation. Follow the wording and spacing of the invitation issued.

Here is an example of a formal dinner invitation:

Mr. and Mrs. Harold Mann
request the pleasure of your company
at dinner
on Thursday, the sixth of June
at half past seven o'clock
980 Park Lane
Walnut Creek
RSVP

A long-form formal acceptance of this invitation, addressed to Mr. and Mrs. Harold Mann, would read

Mr. and Mrs. Norman Phillips (first name is used)
accept with pleasure
the kind invitation of
Mr. and Mrs. Mann (first name is absent)
to dinner
on Thursday, the sixth of June
at half past seven o'clock

The short-form formal acceptance would read the same as the long-form acceptance except that the last three lines ("to dinner . . . seven o'clock") are omitted.

Here is a formal regret reply:

Mr. and Mrs. Norman Phillips
regret that a previous engagement
prevents their accepting
the kind invitation of
Mr. and Mrs. Mann
for Thursday, the sixth of June

Here is an example of a formal reply to a multi-hosted event:

> Miss Elizabeth Coleman
> accepts with pleasure
> the kind invitation of
> Mrs. Gerard and
> Miss Gray and
> Miss Zimmer
> to dinner
> on Tuesday, the tenth of November
> at nine o'clock

A formal reply to an organization event would read

> Miss Elizabeth Coleman
> accepts with pleasure
> the kind invitation of
> the Alpha Chapter of
> Beta Chi Delta
> for Saturday, May the sixth
> at nine o'clock

Keep in mind that an invitation needs to state the specifics of where and when, for whom and why. You should send your acceptance or regret within a week of receiving the invitation, and your decision should not be reversed.

"All children must look after their own upbringing." Parents can only give good advice or put them on the right paths, but the final forming of a person's character lies in their own hands.
—Anne Frank (1929–1945)

XVIII

A LAST WORD ABOUT COURTESY

❧

𝒟o not wear your courtesy like a watch, to be taken out now and then when you want to impress people. Be courteous always, wherever you go, with whomever you happen to be.

Help people feel at ease. Do small kindnesses, share your good feelings with others, and try to overlook casual rudeness in others. Never make another person appear ridiculous or injure his feelings.

Be gentle and kind. Be simple in your tastes and sincere in your actions and let everything you do and say be governed by that timeless rule: "Love your neighbor as yourself, and do unto others as you would have them do unto you" (Galatians 5:14).

Keep in mind that every person on earth carries the Spirit of God in his soul. The fruits of His presence are love, joy, peace, patience, kindness, generosity, faithfulness, gentleness, and self-control.

ACKNOWLEDGMENTS

THE CLASS OF 1950 EXPRESSES ITS SINCERE
APPRECIATION TO THOSE WHOSE TALENT AND
FINANCIAL ASSISTANCE HAVE MADE
THIS BOOK POSSIBLE.

Kay Pepper Altamirano
Pamela Thorsen Amoss
Jennifer Barry Design, Sausalito, California
Carol Monpere Becker
Mary Helen Briscoe
Alda De Prati Cavanna
Susan Wheat Cony
Curtiss Printing
Lillian Machado Dickson
Lady Bug Doherty
Pat Van Obbergh Ewing
Margaret Marks Grasso
Joanne Keig Harris
Ann O'Connor Hogland
Virginia Stewart Jarvis
Marion "Sue" Larkins Kunst
Ann Rogers Lafranchi
Joan English Lane
Isabelle Surcouf Manning

Amy Armstrong Phillips
Lynn Barry Pickart
Elizabeth Chapman Purdom Memorial Fund
Angela Musco Putkey
Nancy Gallot Rembert
Dorris Callaghan Slater
Mariana Casserly Smith
Patricia Butler Thawley
Tilda Muller Thompson
Sister Mary Gervaise Valpey, O.P.
Char Massie Williams
Sally Scott Woodside
Sally Wooster

Winifred Lane was born in 1871 in Salt Lake City, Utah. In 1889 she entered the Dominican Convent of San Rafael and took the name Sister Mercedes.

Sister Mercedes' first teaching assignment was at Saint Rose Academy in San Francisco. She then went to Saint Agnes School in Stockton and later to Saint Vincent Ferrer School in Vallejo.

In 1908 she became headmistress of the Dominican Convent in San Rafael; she also served as head of its English department. During her twenty-five-year tenure as head-mistress, she traveled throughout the United States and Europe to study new teaching methods.

She was dedicated to the formation of spiritually strong, well-educated, and gracious women. Her students were adolescent girls from many of California's leading families as well as students from all parts of the world.

She remained active in the school until 1950, when she retired to the Mother House of the Dominican Convent in San Rafael.

A tall and stately woman, Sister Mercedes is remembered fondly by several generations of students for her sympathetic understanding and the twinkle of joy in her very blue eyes. Her manner expressed gentleness, dignity, graciousness, and humor as she supervised study hall and the refectory, encouraging good posture, good manners, and well-modulated voices.

In 1910 she wrote *A Book of Courtesy,* which was used as a textbook at the school for decades; the students meticulously copied its precepts in manuscript class. Many graduates of Dominican Convent kept their copy of the book when they left school.

When Sister Mercedes died in 1965 at the age of ninety-four, *A Book of Courtesy* was out of print. A small group of the last students to benefit from her presence at the school revised and updated her book in the hope that her spiritual and practical guidance would continue to inspire readers, young and old alike, with her wisdom.